Summary and Analysis of

THE EURO

How a Common Currency Threatens the Future of Europe

Based on the Book
by Joseph E. Stiglitz

WORTH BOOKS
SMART SUMMARIES

All rights reserved, including without limitation the right to reproduce this book or any portion thereof in any form or by any means, whether electronic or mechanical, now known or hereinafter invented, without the express written permission of the publisher.

This Worth Books book is based on the 2016 hardcover edition of *The Euro* by Joseph E. Stiglitz, published by W. W. Norton & Company.

Summary and analysis copyright © 2017 by Open Road Integrated Media, Inc.

ISBN: 978-1-5040-4658-9

Worth Books
180 Maiden Lane
Suite 8A
New York, NY 10038
www.worthbooks.com

Worth Books is a division of Open Road Integrated Media, Inc.

The summary and analysis in this book are meant to complement your reading experience and bring you closer to a great work of nonfiction. This book is not intended as a substitute for the work that it summarizes and analyzes, and it is not authorized, approved, licensed, or endorsed by the work's author or publisher. Worth Books makes no representations or warranties with respect to the accuracy or completeness of the contents of this book.

Contents

Context	1
Overview	3
Summary	9
Timeline	25
Cast of Characters	27
Direct Quotes and Analysis	31
Trivia	35
What's That Word?	37
Critical Response	41
About Joseph E. Stiglitz	43
For Your Information	45
Bibliography	49

Context

The Euro, written by Nobel Prize–winning economist Joseph E. Stiglitz, was released in August 2016, during a lull in the eurozone crisis. Yet these were not calm times; Europe itself was at a moment of dramatic change. The influx of refugees from the Middle East was testing European integration, creating significant political headwinds for German Chancellor Angela Merkel, who had recently admitted around one million emigrants into Germany. Meanwhile, Britain's vote on June 23rd to exit the European Union continued to send shockwaves around the world. On July 13, Theresa May became Prime Minister of the United Kingdom, promising to enact the British exit, or Brexit, in 2017.

SUMMARY AND ANALYSIS

Further global economic and political uncertainty continued to cloud the outlook for Europe as reservations created by the United States' 2016 presidential race seeped into European minds. Amidst all of these dramatic political events, the eurozone continued to endure anemic economic growth. While the United States had begun to truly recover from the 2008 financial crisis, mid-2016 the eurozone seemed to still be mired in relative stagnation.

Overview

In *The Euro,* Stiglitz argues that the fundamental cause of the eurozone's recent economic difficulties was the creation of a single currency without the institutions to support it. The euro bound together 19 countries with very different economies (and very different views about economics), but it did not include the institutions or rules to make such a union succeed. The results of this union are clear: Although the United States has experienced growth since the 2008 financial crisis, Europe is stagnant, and eurozone unemployment remains over 10%. Even Germany, held up as a model for other European countries, is growing at a meager average of 0.8% per year. Greece, Italy, Ireland, Finland, and Portugal have seen their

SUMMARY AND ANALYSIS

GDP shrink more during the euro crisis than during the Great Depression.

A core problem is that the euro is not flexible. The value of the US dollar is correlated to the health of the US economy, but the value of the euro is correlated to the health of 19 different economies. Imagine if the United States were undergoing an economic contraction. The value of the dollar would fall, making American goods cheaper for foreigners and foreign goods more expensive for Americans. This adjustment would encourage foreigners to buy American goods—helping US employment and eventually leading to a recovery. Greece's currency, the euro, cannot adjust solely to Greece's specific situation, so a process of internal devaluation in Greece must instead take place. That means lower wages for Greek workers and lower prices for Greek products. Yet this is hardly a solution comparable to the traditional exchange rate mechanism. Under internal devaluation, Greeks with debts who take a pay cut find it harder to pay off their debts. The Greek government, already strapped for cash, in turn takes in less in tax receipts, which further weakens its position.

The weakness of the Greek government endangers its banks. The United States has a national bank deposit scheme, so bank deposits in Montana are just as protected as those in the wealthier state of New York. This is not true in Europe—each member of the eurozone has its own separate deposit insurance. In the United States, if there were a crisis and banks had to be capitalized, the federal government could theoretically print an unlimited amount of money to backstop its banking system. Greece (or any other eurozone country) cannot do this. Therefore, as Greek banks lost more and more of their capital, they became weaker and weaker, creating a vicious cycle.

While the euro was supposed to bring together countries like Germany and Greece, economically tightening their bonds, the inflexibility of a partial union actually pushed them apart. The eurozone currently does not have the tools to deal with these issues, partly because European institutions account for a very small amount of spending in Europe.

In contrast, although American states share the same currency, they are stitched much closer together than EU member nations. The EU's spending is equal to around 1% of GDP, while in the United States, federal spending is around 20%. If California is booming and South Dakota has economic problems, South Dakotans will receive federal government assistance, and can also easily move to another state with a stronger economy. In the United States, the national language is English, the culture of each state is relatively similar, and federal regulations are homogenous. This is not the case in Europe. A Greek who wants to move to Paris needs to not only learn French, but needs to adapt to a very different culture and a new set of laws. This makes it harder for the average citizen to emigrate, especially after an economic nosedive.

The fatally flawed design of the euro has had a detrimental effect on other related policies. For example, the European Central Bank (ECB), which controls the euro, has a mandate to focus only on preventing inflation. The US Federal Reserve, on the other hand, also focuses on economic stability, growth, and full employment. The ECB's sole focus on preventing inflation has skewed policy and resulted in extra unemployment.

Another major problem has been the austerity policies forced upon certain countries like Greece and Spain. Instead of pro-growth policies, the Troika (a group made up of the European Commission, the ECB, and the International Monetary Fund) has forced these countries to raise tax rates and slash government spending. This results in lower take-home pay for workers, which damages the economy when people have less to spend on goods and services. Lower spending, in turn, results in a weaker economy. Higher taxes encourage greater tax avoidance, while the combination of these failed policies further encourages skilled labor to emigrate. Austerity policies are hurting Europe's recovery, and should be replaced with increased government spending and the forgiveness of some debt.

Stiglitz believes that the best solution to all of these problems is "more Europe." The eurozone should create a banking union so all eurozone banks are backstopped by the ECB, instead of by separate national governments. Debt should be issued at a eurozone-wide level, potentially through the proposed "Eurobonds." The eurozone should implement structural reforms, such as improved bankruptcy laws, reduced tax competition between eurozone member states, and automatic stimulus in case of a crisis. The ECB must also be reformed to focus on full employment and economic growth, instead of its current mandate to simply combat inflation.

A less preferred, but still workable option, is "less Europe." This means one or more countries leaving the eurozone. If Greece left, it could implement an electronic currency that would allow it to replace the euro and would lead to a greater ability to collect taxes. Greece could implement a system of trade tokens, sometimes known as "Buffett chits." Essentially, this would require imports to be in proportion to exports, resulting in a trade balance or surplus, thus creating long-term stability. Another option involves Germany, and perhaps other northern European member countries, leaving the eurozone, which would minimize some of the economic contradictions inherent in the single currency.

SUMMARY AND ANALYSIS

A fourth option is the "flexible euro." This would allow Greece or other crisis-hit countries to keep the euro in name while making the value of the euro in one country different than that in another. This system would also be electronic, and would also involve a solidarity fund to more equitably share the costs of economic adjustment. It would include greater investment in struggling countries and a revamped financial system that could eliminate negative externalities and predatory finance.

Although each of these solutions would improve Europe's situation, the current political climate suggests that a continuation of today's expensive, harmful policies is more likely. The fundamental problem is a continued belief in failed neoliberal policies that are not only exacerbating Europe's economic problems, but also creating new ones. The actions taken against crisis-hit countries like Greece and Spain are the result of discredited, blame-the-victim economic policies. Saving the euro is important, and it still can be saved. However, it must be done in a way that promotes true convergence and economic growth, avoids failed neoliberal policies, focuses on bringing back employment, and promotes true prosperity and integration across the eurozone.

Summary

Part I: Europe in Crisis

1. The Euro Crisis

Stiglitz begins by discussing the euro crisis, arguing that the euro's flawed design is the fundamental cause of Europe's current economic problems. The euro is the currency of 19 countries, each with a different economic situation. Because the currency is not flexible, crisis-hit countries like Greece are unable to devalue their currency during hard times.

Not only was the design of the euro flawed from the beginning, but the austerity policies enacted

SUMMARY AND ANALYSIS

as a response to the euro crisis—generally higher taxes and lower government spending—made the situation worse by stunting growth. These policies were enacted due to neoliberal "market fundamentalism," a belief that the market is always right and government has little to no role in shaping economic policy.

To solve the crisis, there should either be "more Europe" (greater economic integration between eurozone members) or "less Europe" (a partial unraveling of the euro project). Regardless of the solution chosen, the current path is extremely costly and unsustainable.

2. The Euro: The Hope and the Reality

The euro was founded on three interrelated principles:

1. Uniting Europe economically and politically.
2. Increasing economic growth due to tighter integration.
3. Peace due to economic prosperity and political integration.

Given Europe's tumultuous and bloody history during the first half of the 20th century, these interrelated goals were seen as vital by the founders of the eurozone. They had hoped that a united Europe would be more influential and powerful on the world stage, but, in reality, the EU only has true influence on a limited number of issues where there is a broad consensus among member states.

Economic integration can be achieved without a common currency. The United States and Canada, for example, have had a free trade deal since 1988 and have very codependent economies. Although the euro was a noble goal, an integrated economic system without agreement on how the economy should be managed is unsustainable. Economic integration that outpaces political integration is a major problem, and while the eurozone is economically integrated, it is quite divided politically. Moreover, the euro has created a "democratic deficit" in which democratically elected governments such as Greece have been forced to accept policies they oppose. Their economy and membership in the eurozone is held hostage by the powerful European Central Bank, which is not democratically elected and is heavily influenced by powerful countries like Germany.

3. Europe's Dismal Performance

The eurozone has performed poorly during the post-financial crisis period. Germany, held up by some as a model of European growth, has only grown by 6.8%

since 2007, an extremely low growth rate by historical standards. Other countries, such as Spain, Italy, and Portugal, have seen GDP fall by levels that rival or exceed the contractions they experienced during the Great Depression. Countries like Germany have blamed these problems on corruption, profligate spending, inefficient labor markets, and the like. Yet it was the euro's lack of flexibility that made it impossible for countries to adapt to changing economic circumstances, and has therefore caused much of the eurozone's financial pain. It is important to note that while the economic problems are the most visible, other indirect effects, such as a spike in suicides, reveals the truly devastating cost of the failure of the eurozone.

Part II: Flawed from the Start

4. When Can a Single Currency Ever Work?

Many people have looked to the United States and argued that if it can have a single currency, so can Europe. However, the United States is much more united in terms of culture, language, and legal regulations, making the US model inapplicable for Europe. Because the euro makes a country-specific devaluation of currency impossible, many believed that internal devaluation—lower prices of labor, goods, or services—on a country-specific basis would fill in the gap. Stiglitz shows that while internal devaluation has occurred, it has not been an adequate substitute for the exchange rate mechanism. Perniciously, internal devaluation results in lower GDP and hurts workers who have to settle for lower wages.

Furthermore, Europeans tended to emphasize fiscal deficits instead of trade deficits. In the 1990s, many believed that trade deficits were caused by excessive government spending, but now we know they are caused by the private sector. Moreover, eurozone countries are limited to a fiscal deficit of 3% of GDP, which means they are not able to spend their way out of a crisis.

Currencies that are fixed and inflexible—as is the euro—are prone to crisis because they lack a proper exchange rate mechanism.

The euro has created a peculiar situation in which a country borrowing in its own currency exposes itself to the risk of being unable to repay its debts. If, for example, the United States is in debt, it can always print the money that it owes. Greece, on the other hand, cannot freely print euros, and is thus stuck with crushing levels of debt. While it was believed the euro would create convergence among economies in Europe, it has, in reality, pushed them apart.

SUMMARY AND ANALYSIS

5. The Euro: A Divergent System

Many believed that the euro would foster convergence among economies; in reality the opposite was true—it created divergence. For example, even though Greek and German banks both do business in euros, money has flowed out of Greek banks toward German ones, as most believe German banks are more stable than their Greek counterparts. The weaker banks thus become less well-capitalized. If there was a common deposit insurance scheme across the eurozone, this problem would be eliminated, yet Germany opposes it, believing that it would essentially amount to rich countries bailing out poor countries. The German government argues that common standards and rules are necessary as a precondition to common deposit insurance.

The common euro system has also led to a regulatory race to the bottom as countries compete to attract business by offering the least regulation. Since every eurozone country has the same access to the single market, but each country has separate regulations, this encourages individual countries to lower their standards in order to attract businesses that can base themselves in lightly regulated areas and sell products or financial services to areas with stricter regulations.

The free movement of labor also exacerbates the problem, as skilled high-earning individuals leave crisis-hit countries for other areas of the eurozone. Not only does this hurt the ability of indebted countries to pay back their debts, it increases the incentives for other workers to leave, as only the workers who remain are responsible for the increased taxes needed to supply government services and pay off the immense debt.

Further causes of divergence include the austerity policies—such as higher taxes and lower government spending—adopted as a response to the crisis, the lack of investment in infrastructure and other areas by poorer countries, the lack of wealth of certain eurozone countries, and the differing rates of adopting technologies. Although common Eurobonds—bonds jointly issued by all eurozone members—could solve some of the problems of divergence, they are adamantly opposed by a group of countries led by Germany. Further austerity and economic reforms imposed to alleviate the crisis may only make it worse.

6. Monetary Policy and the European Central Bank

Although the European Central Bank has been fundamentally flawed since its inception, it has done some good, particularly in 2012, when the head of the institution, Mario Draghi, declared that the ECB would do "whatever it takes" to save the euro.

SUMMARY AND ANALYSIS

A key flaw of the ECB is its mandate to focus solely on taming inflation. By contrast, the American Federal Reserve addresses both unemployment and financial stability in addition to inflation. This singular focus on inflation has restricted the ECB from helping alleviate unemployment, which has, in turn, permanently lowered economic growth in Europe. Combating inflation instead of joblessness prioritizes creditors over debtors and employers over job seekers, which increases inequality. While it is often believed that the ECB is not and should not be a political institution, the reality is that the choices made by the ECB are political decisions. The decision not to bail out Greek banks was political in nature, just as was the decision to make the ECB independent. In reality, no institution is truly independent. The ECB is largely staffed by financial professionals with their own agendas, while other voices affected by ECB decisions—like labor—are absent.

In the modern era, many different theories of monetary policy have been ultimately discarded. Monetarism, the belief that the monetary supply should be increased at a fixed rate, was popular; however, it led to the US recession of the early 1980s and a lost decade in Latin America. Inflation targeting, the belief that the central bank should focus solely on inflation, took the place of monetarism, yet it too has proven unworkable, as shown by the ECB's failed inflation-only mandate, which resulted in higher unemployment. Quantitative easing, essentially the printing of money as a form of economic stimulus, which had only a limited impact in the United States, fared even worse in Europe because other countries were already doing it, and emerging market countries had begun to protect themselves from competitive devaluations.

Part III: Misconceived Policies

7. Crises Policies: How Troika Policies Compounded the Flawed Eurozone Structure, Ensuring Depression

The euro was built on shaky foundations, and the policies enacted to fix the euro crisis have only exacerbated the problem. Instead of focusing on growth in crisis-hit countries, the economically stronger countries forced austerity programs on the hard-hit countries, making it even more of a challenge for them to recover from crisis. For example, the Troika pressured Greece into adopting measures that make it almost impossible for cash-strapped Greeks to protect their houses from foreclosure. This policy won't fix the economy; it will merely put families on the street. Austerity is not only a flawed policy but an ideological attempt to minimize government and its role in the economy.

Austerity primarily consists of increased taxes, reduced spending, and the privatization of certain sectors of the economy. Of course, reduced spending and higher taxes simply compound the economic malaise. Moreover, the system implemented in Greece, which includes paying taxes ahead of time, simply encourages more tax evasion and hurts small businesses.

Germany has consistently opposed a realistic debt restructuring for Greece, yet some believe that Greece should go ahead with or without German approval. Indeed, Argentina grew rapidly after its own restructuring. Stiglitz argues that a more realistic proposal, with sensible structural reforms, some debt write-offs, and a lower primary surplus requirement, would have helped Greece much more than austerity. Most academics agree that austerity is a flawed policy and that the austerity policies imposed on Greece have exacerbated its downturn.

8. Structural Reforms That Further Compounded Failure

In return for financial assistance during the crisis, the Troika demanded structural reforms to the economies of crisis-hit countries. These so-called reforms were often counterproductive, outright harmful, or simply a waste of time. For example, the Troika demanded Greece change its laws regarding uniform bread loaf size and what qualifies as fresh milk. More disconcerting, the Troika curtailed workers' rights through labor reforms. It would be better, Stiglitz argues, to adopt an industrial policy that steers crisis-hit economies toward productive industries instead of simply relying on the market to lead to economic growth. A focus on fighting inequality and distributing political and economic power equitably would also promote lasting growth.

Furthermore, reforms to the financial sector, including greater oversight to prevent financial crises in the first place, are crucial. Finally, committing to fight climate change is not only a moral and ecological imperative, it is also sound economically. For example, Spain and Greece have the ability to produce wind and solar power that could be exported to other countries in Europe.

Adopting an agenda that promotes growth, instead of the austerity measures that restrict it, could mean a healthier Europe. Unfortunately, austerity has ruled European policy, resulting in higher unemployment and anemic growth.

Part IV: A Way Forward?

9. Creating a Eurozone That Works

To fix the eurozone's economic problems, Stiglitz argues for either "more Europe" or "less Europe." To achieve "more Europe," the following changes are necessary:

SUMMARY AND ANALYSIS

- A banking union complete with common deposit insurance to prevent bank runs in weaker countries.
- The "mutualization of debt," such as through jointly issued Eurobonds, to help prevent divergence between the fortunes of weaker and stronger eurozone members.
- A "common framework for stability" that includes a fund for common action, improved budget rules, automatic stimulus in the case of a downturn, better regulation of the economy, and other steps to ensure stability in the eurozone.
- A "true convergence policy" that discourages surpluses and simultaneously increases wages in creditor countries like Germany.
- Changing the mandate of the ECB to focus on full employment and economic growth, not only on controlling inflation.
- Adopting further structural reforms, including an expedited bankruptcy process, corporate governance reforms, the promotion of investments in the environment, and financial reforms to ensure stability and long-term prosperity.
- A "commitment to shared prosperity," including limiting tax competition between member states and making redistribution a supranational, European-level responsibility.

In addition to these reforms, further "crisis policy" reforms are necessary, including growth policies, ditching austerity, and restructuring the debts of crisis-hit states that are unable to move past crushing levels of debt.

10. Can There Be an Amicable Divorce?

Although Stiglitz believes "more Europe" would solve the eurozone's problems, these reforms may never be implemented for political reasons. If they are not, a "less Europe" strategy would involve several important steps.

Leaving the euro, a crisis-hit country such as Greece could convert to an e-payment system, eliminating paper currency and allowing the country to return to the drachma without a lag period. Moreover, this would result in improved ability to collect taxes. After a divorce, Greece would restore its ability to create credit. This would allow Greece to create a new, accountable system that prevents bankers and financial institutions from irresponsible actions, which would exploit investors, the poor, and national governments.

A trade token system, sometimes known as "Buffett chits" (or tokens), would require chits in proportion to exports, resulting in a trade balance or a trade surplus. Exporters would be granted one token for each euro worth of goods exported. Importers would need to pay one token for each euro worth of goods imported. This would create a market in tokens, but since the supply of imported goods could not outweigh the supply of exports, Greece would experience long-term stability. Furthermore, debt restructuring of Greece would help set it on the path to prosperity.

Alternatively, Germany and other northern European countries could leave the euro, minimizing many of the problems and contradictions inherent in the common currency.

11. Toward a Flexible Euro

Although Stiglitz believes "more Europe" is the best strategy to fix the eurozone's problems, moving toward a system with a flexible euro is another workable strategy. Countries would change to an electronic system, allowing flexible euro exchange rates by country.

To stabilize the relative exchange rates between eurozone countries, the following steps could be taken:

- Germany and other surplus countries could balance their trade through a chit system (as described in the previous chapter).
- The burdens of economic adjustment could be shared more efficiently by all members,

instead of being primarily imposed on deficit countries.
- More investment in struggling countries, including infrastructure investment and a solidarity fund, would help close the productivity gap.

Fundamentally, regulators need to improve oversight over economic matters and actively work toward a fairer system that eliminates negative externalities, i.e., the harmful effects experienced by disadvantaged people who have no voice in making these economic decisions. Although some want to return to a time when there were fewer regulations in the economy, this will only lead to financial crisis or disaster. Eventually, once sufficient harmonization and convergence has been achieved, this flexible euro strategy could allow Europe to have a true, successful single currency.

12. The Way Forward

Though the previous three chapters discussed Stiglitz's solutions to the euro crisis, he pessimistically believes it is unlikely that any of them will be implemented. Instead, the pressure will build until one or more countries leave the eurozone.

Usually, creditors want to make it possible for their debtors to pay back their loans. So why did Germany implement policies that actually made it harder for Greece to repay its debts? The root cause is a belief in discredited economics and blame-the-victim ideology. Fundamentally, arguments over austerity and the euro are a fight about power and ideology, which have been forced upon countries like Greece. Not only is this bad policy, it is undemocratic. Neoliberalism has failed in the United States, resulting in economic stagnation for most people and rising incomes only for those at the top. These same trends are playing out in Europe. Despite these headwinds, saving the European project is extremely important. Europe was the birthplace of the enlightenment, and it continues to be a strong voice in the fight for human rights and democratic values. The euro can be saved, but it must be done in a way that creates prosperity for all.

Timeline

February 7, 1992: The Maastricht Treaty is signed, officially creating the European Union.

January 1, 1999: The euro is introduced.

January 1, 2002: Euro coins and currency are introduced.

2008: A worldwide financial crisis rocks the globe. The US government creates a $700 billion assistance package to shore up its financial system.

October 2009: Eurozone unemployment breaches 10%.

SUMMARY AND ANALYSIS

December 2009: Worries about Greece build, forcing the Prime Minister to argue that Greece was "not about to default on its debts."

2010: The first of many austerity packages is accepted by the Greek government.

July 5, 2015: Greeks vote against further austerity. Despite this vote, the leaders in the Greek government eventually buckle to pressure to accept the deal, for which they are later re-elected.

Cast of Characters

Ben Shalom Bernanke: Chairman of the Federal Reserve from 2006–2014 who helped lead the United States through the 2008 financial crisis.

Milton Friedman: Famous economist, Nobel Prize winner, and staunch advocate of free markets.

Herbert Hoover: US president whose austerity policies transformed a stock market crash into a depression, according to Stiglitz.

SUMMARY AND ANALYSIS

John Maynard Keynes: Famous economist and father of Keynesian economics, for which Stiglitz is an advocate.

Helmut Josef Michael Kohl: Chancellor of Germany from 1982–1998, and key player in the Maastricht Treaty, which created the European Union.

François Mitterrand: French president from 1981–1995, instrumental in the creation of the Maastricht Treaty.

George Papandreou: Prime minister of Greece from 2009–2011. His tenure was consumed with, and eventually ended by, the economic crisis in Greece.

Antonis Samaras: The prime minister of Greece from 2012–2015.

Wolfgang Schäuble: Germany's minister of finance under Angela Merkel, seen as a staunch advocate of austerity policies.

Jean-Claude Trichet: President of the European Central Bank from 2003–2011.

Alexis Tsipras: The young prime minister of Greece who famously called a referendum to determine whether Greece should accept further austerity. Although austerity was voted down, his government eventually buckled and accepted a deal.

Yanis Varoufakis: The controversial and blunt Greek minster of finance under Tsipras, who argued forcefully against austerity.

Direct Quotes and Analysis

"A main argument of this book is that the euro has deepened the divide—has resulted in the weaker countries becoming weaker and the stronger countries becoming stronger."

In the preface to this book, Stiglitz lays out his case directly, arguing that the euro has not increased convergence as was hoped, but has in fact led to further divergence among eurozone countries, tearing them apart and increasing income inequality.

"The eurozone created a new situation. Countries and firms and households within countries borrowed in euros. But though they were borrowing in the cur-

rency they used, it was a currency that they did not control."

Even though Greece was borrowing money in its own currency—the euro—it lacked the ability to make any necessary adjustments to that currency to help alleviate its economic woes. This problem is a key cause of many of the problems facing eurozone countries in economic crisis.

"It is preposterous that the Troika held an entire country hostage over things like this."

Stiglitz rails against the Troika's demand that Greece change its regulations regarding the size of bread loaves, arguing it is an unimportant issue that, along with other pointless regulations, betrays ulterior motives amongst those trying to "help" Greece.

"The euro can and should be saved—but not at any cost."

Although he criticizes the euro repeatedly throughout this book, Stiglitz in fact believes the euro can help Europe. However, he cautions that this will only work if the system is structured properly. If it continues to be mismanaged, the costs will greatly outweigh the benefits.

THE EURO

"Too often, it seemed as if saving the banks, or even just the euro, was given precedence over human welfare."

Stiglitz criticizes the vested interests that prioritized economic theory over the lives of average people in crisis-hit countries. Policies like internal devaluation have led to real deprivation among working-class Europeans.

Trivia

1. The European Union began as the European Coal and Steel Community in 1952, before morphing to its current status as a union of independent nations.

2. The euro is also used in South America—in French Guiana, the French overseas region.

3. The European Central Bank announced on May 4, 2016 that the 500 euro note—one of the world's most valuable banknotes—would be phased out by 2018 due to fears over its use in black market transactions.

SUMMARY AND ANALYSIS

4. France was the first country to produce euro coins.

5. Although former Prime Minister Tony Blair had plans for his country to join the single currency, Britain never adopted the euro and continues to use the pound instead.

6. The nineteen countries in the original Eurozone are: Austria, Belgium, Cyprus, Estonia, Finland, France, Germany, Greece, Ireland, Italy, Latvia, Lithuania, Luxembourg, Malta, the Netherlands, Portugal, Slovakia, Slovenia, and Spain.

What's That Word?

Common deposit insurance: Deposit insurance administered across all members of the eurozone and guaranteed by the European Central Bank.

Democratic deficit: The lack of democratic accountability inherent in the current structure of supranational institutions such as the ECB.

Eurozone: The group of 19 countries that have adopted the euro as their currency.

Fiscal deficit: A deficit caused by spending more money than is raised.

SUMMARY AND ANALYSIS

Keynesianism: An economic theory that proposes government spending as a way to fight economic downturns. Stiglitz is considered a Keynesian.

"Less Europe": Decreased economic and political integration between eurozone members.

Market fundamentalism: A pejorative term for neoliberalism.

"More Europe": Increased economic and political integration between eurozone members.

Negative externality: A negative consequence of an action suffered by people not involved in the original action. For example, bicyclists suffer from pollution created by cars.

Neoliberalism: An economic school of thought that generally opposes government regulation, supports free trade, supports austerity, and is opposed to Keynesianism.

"Third way": An economic philosophy advocating limited but important government intervention in an otherwise largely free market economy.

Trade deficit: A deficit caused by exporting goods less valuable than those imported.

Troika: A group made up of the European Commission, the European Central Bank, and the International Monetary Fund. The Troika is responsible for monitoring the euro crisis.

Critical Response

"A cogent and urgent argument of compelling interest to economists and policymakers." —*Kirkus Reviews*

"Stiglitz's critique of specific policies is original and extremely helpful." —*The Financial Times*

"The final message of the book is clear and widely shared: we need 'more Europe' with risk-sharing, fiscal transfers and more political integration (the solution that Stiglitz seems to prefer) or 'less Europe' following an 'amicable divorce' or a 'flexible euro'—but the status quo is untenable."
—*Times Higher Education*

SUMMARY AND ANALYSIS

"Mr. Stiglitz is at his best when coolly analytical . . . on the essentials, he is surely right. Without a radical overhaul of its workings, the euro seems all but certain to fail." —*The Economist*

"*The Euro* is a useful prescient look at the near future of the European Union."
—Hazel Henderson, SeekingAlpha.com

About Joseph E. Stiglitz

Recipient of the 2001 Nobel Memorial Prize in Economic Sciences, Joseph E. Stiglitz was born in Gary, Indiana, in 1943. Coincidentally, the first winner of the Nobel Prize in Economics, Paul Samuelson, was also born in Gary. Stiglitz grew up in a political family, and often discussed economic and civil rights issues with his parents. After attending Amherst College and MIT, he completed his postgraduate work at the University of Chicago and MIT. He graduated with his PhD from the latter, where he studied under four Nobel Prize–winning professors.

In the 1980s, Stiglitz calculated the damages suffered by Native Americans in a land dispute, and also spoke out against the Reagan administration's efforts

SUMMARY AND ANALYSIS

to sell oilfields for far less than Stiglitz calculated them to be worth. In the early 1990s, Stiglitz joined the Clinton administration as the Chairman of the Council of Economic Advisers. Stiglitz helped define the "third way" economic philosophy of limited government and managed markets.

Stiglitz has taught at various institutions, including Stanford, Oxford, Yale, Princeton, and Columbia, where he currently teaches. In 2011 Stiglitz was named one of *Time*'s 100 most influential people in the world.

In 2016, Stiglitz waded into the controversial US presidential election, claiming Donald Trump deserved an F on economic issues. Joseph Stiglitz lives in New York City.

For Your Information

Online
"The 1 Percent's Problem." VanityFair.com
"Joseph Stiglitz Asks, 'Can the Euro Be Saved?'" Wnyc.org
"Joseph Stiglitz on Brexit, Europe's Long Cycle of Crisis, and Why German Economics Is Different." QZ.com
"Reform or Divorce in Europe." Project-Syndicate.org
"Stiglitz Grades Donald Trump an F on Economics." Bloomberg.com
"The problem with Europe is the euro." TheGuardian.com

SUMMARY AND ANALYSIS

Books

Global Inequality: A New Approach for the Age of Globalization by Branko Milanovic

The Go-Go Years: The Drama and Crashing Finale of Wall Street's Bullish 60s by John Brooks

Greed and Glory on Wall Street: The Fall of the House of Lehman by Ken Auletta

Rewriting the Rules of the American Economy: An Agenda for Growth and Shared Prosperity by Joseph E. Stiglitz

The Rise and Fall of American Growth: The U.S. Standard of Living Since The Civil War by Robert J. Gordon

Slippery Slope: Europe's Troubled Future by Giles Merritt

A Student's Guide to Economics: ISI Guides to the Major Disciplines by Paul Heyne

The Traders by Donny Kleinfield

Welcome to the Poisoned Chalice: The Destruction of Greece and the Future of Europe by James K. Galbraith

Other Books by Joseph E. Stiglitz

Freefall: America, Free Markets, and the Sinking of the World Economy Globalization and Its Discontents

The Great Divide: Unequal Societies and What We Can Do About Them Making Globalization Work

THE EURO

The Price of Inequality: How Today's Divided Society Endangers Our Future

Rewriting the Rules of the American Economy: An Agenda for Growth and Shared Prosperity

Bibliography

Curran, Enda and Angie Lau. "Stiglitz Grades Donald Trump an F on Economics." *Bloomberg*. September 18, 2016. http://www.bloomberg.com/news/articles/2016-09-19/stiglitz-grades-trump-f-on-economics-cites-china-trade-war-risk.

"Joseph E. Stiglitz – Biographical." *The Sveriges Riksbank Prize in Economic Sciences in Memory of Alfred Nobel 2001.* http://www.nobelprize.org/nobel_prizes/economic-sciences/laureates/2001/stiglitz-bio.html.

Kampfner, John. "The Euro and Its Threat to the Future of Europe by Joseph Stiglitz – review." *The Guardian*. August 22, 2016. https://www.theguardian.com/books/2016/aug/22/the-euro-

and-its-threat-to-the-future-of-europe-joseph-stiglitz-review.

Lowenstein, Roger. "Nobel Laureate Joseph Stiglitz Says the Euro Needs Big Reform." *The New York Times.* August 16, 2016. http://www.nytimes.com/2016/08/21/books/review/euro-joseph-e-stiglitz.html.

Quaglia, Lucia. "The Euro and Its Threat to the Future of Europe, by Joseph Stiglitz." *Times Higher Education.* September 1, 2016. https://www.timeshighereducation.com/books/review-the-euro-and-its-threat-to-the-future-of-europe-joseph-stiglitz-allen-lane.

Sandbu, Martin. "'The Euro: And its Threat to the Future of Europe', by Joseph Stiglitz" *The Financial Times.* August 5, 2016. http://www.ft.com/cms/s/0/a84ae368-5a2e-11e6-9f70-badea1b336d4.html.

Thorne, Nick. "Letter from French Guiana: EU west." *The Guardian.* March 5, 2013. https://www.theguardian.com/world/2013/mar/05/letter-from-french-guiana-france.

WORTH BOOKS
SMART SUMMARIES

So much to read, so little time?

Explore summaries of bestselling fiction and essential nonfiction books on a variety of subjects, including business, history, science, lifestyle, and much more.

**Visit the store at
www.ebookstore.worthbooks.com**

MORE SMART SUMMARIES
FROM WORTH BOOKS

CURRENT AFFAIRS

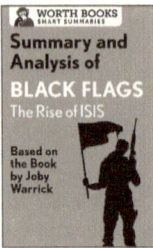
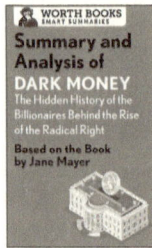

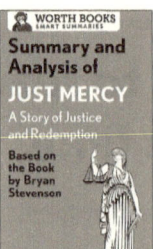
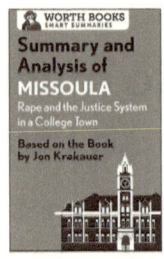
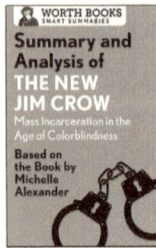
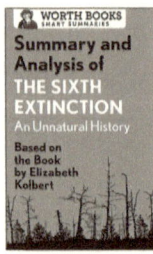

Find a full list of our authors and
titles at www.openroadmedia.com

FOLLOW US
@OpenRoadMedia

www.ingramcontent.com/pod-product-compliance
Lightning Source LLC
Chambersburg PA
CBHW060343080526
44584CB00013B/898